# Last Poems

## By

## Laurence Hope

**Fredonia Books**
**Amsterdam, The Netherlands**

Last Poems

by
Laurence Hope

ISBN: 1-58963-622-8

Copyright © 2001 by Fredonia Books

Fredonia Books
Amsterdam, the Netherlands
http://www.fredoniabooks.com

All rights reserved, including the right to reproduce this book, or portions thereof, in any form.

# Last Poems

## The Masters

Oh, Masters, you who rule the world,
  Will you not wait with me awhile,
When swords are sheathed and sails are furled,
  And all the fields with harvest smile?
I would not waste your time for long,
  I ask you but, when you are tired,
To read how by the weak, the strong
  Are weighed and worshipped and desired.

When weary of the Mart, the Loom,
  The Withering-house, the Rifle-blocks,
The Barrack-square, the Engine-room,
  The pick-axe, ringing on the rocks,—
When tents are pitched and work is done,
  While restful twilight broods above,
By fresh-lit lamp, or dying sun,
  See in my songs how women love.

We shared your lonely watch by night,
  We knew you faithful at the helm,
Our thoughts went with you through the fight
  That saved a soul,—or wrecked a realm.

Ah, how our hearts leapt forth to you,
  In pride and joy, when you prevailed,
And when you died, serene and true:
  —We wept in silence when you failed!

  Oh, brain, that did not gain the gold!
    Oh, arm, that could not wield the sword
  Here is the love, that is not sold,
    Here are the hearts to hail you Lord!

You played and lost the game? What then?
  The rules are harsh and hard we know,
You, still, oh, brothers, are the men
  Whom we in secret reverence so.
Your work was waste? Maybe your share
  Lay in the hour you laughed and kissed;
Who knows but what your son shall wear
  The laurels that his father missed?

Ay, you who win, and you who lose,
  Whether you triumph,—or despair,—
When your returning footsteps choose
  The homeward track, our love is there.
For, since the world is ordered thus,
  To you the fame, the stress, the sword,
We can but wait, until to us
  You give yourselves, for our reward.

To Whaler's deck and Coral beach,
    To lonely Ranch and Frontier-Fort,
Beyond the narrow bounds of speech
    I lay the cable of my thought.
I fain would send my thanks to you,
    (Though who am I, to give you praise?)
Since what you are, and work you do,
    Are lessons for our easier ways.

    'Neath alien stars your camp-fires glow,
        I know you not,—your tents are far.
    My hope is but in song to show,
        How honoured and how dear you are

## I Shall Forget

Although my life, which thou hast scarred and shaken
   Retains awhile some influence of thee,
As shells, by faithless waves long since forsaken,
   Still murmur with the music of the Sea,

I shall forget. Not thine the haunting beauty,
   Which, once beheld, for ever holds the heart,
Or, if resigned from stress of Fate or Duty,
   Takes part of life away:—the dearer part.

I gave thee love; thou gavest but Desire.
   Ah, the delusion of that summer night!
Thy soul vibrated at the rate of Fire;
   Mine, with the rhythm of the waves of Light.

It is my love for thee that I regret,
Not thee, thyself, and hence,—I shall forget!

# The Lament of Yasmini,
## the Dancing-Girl

Ah, what hast thou done with that Lover of mine?
　　The Lover who only cared for thee?
Mine for a handful of nights, and thine
　　For the Nights that Are and the Days to Be,
The scent of the Champa lost its sweet—
　　So sweet it was in the Times that Were!—
Since His alone, of the numerous feet
　　That climb my steps, have returned not there.
　　　　Ahi, Yasmini, return not there!

Art thou yet athrill at the touch of His hand,
　　Art thou still athirst for His waving hair?
Nay, passion thou never couldst understand,
　　Life's heights and depths thou wouldst never dare.
The Great Things left thee untouched, unmoved,
　　The Lesser Things had thy constant care.
Ah, what hast thou done with the Lover I loved,
　　Who found me wanting, and thee so fair?
　　　　Ahi, Yasmini, He found her fair!

Nay, nay, the greatest of all was thine;
　　The love of the One whom I craved for so,

But much I doubt if thou couldst divine
   The Grace and Glory of Love, or know
The worth of the One whom thine arms embraced.
   I may misjudge thee, but who can tell?
So hard it is, for the one displaced,
   To weigh the worth of a rival's spell.
      Ahi, Yasmini, thy rival's spell!

And Thou, whom I loved: have the seasons brought
   That fair content, which allured Thee so?
Is it all that Thy delicate fancy wrought?
   Yasmini wonders; she may not know.
Yet never the Stars desert the sky,
   To fade away in the desolate Dawn,
But Yasmini watches their glory die,
   And mourns for her own Bright Star withdrawn.
      Ahi, Yasmini, the lonely dawn!

Ah, never the lingering gold dies down
   In a sunset flare of resplendent light,
And never the palm-tree's feathery crown
   Uprears itself to the shadowy night,
But Yasmini thinks of those evenings past,
   When she prayed the glow of the glimmering West
To vanish quickly, that night, at last,
   Might bring Thee back to her waiting breast.
      Ahi, Yasmini, how sweet that rest!

Yet I would not say that I always weep;
   The force, that made such a desperate thing
Of my love for Thee, has not fallen asleep,
   The blood still leaps, and the senses sing,
While other passion has oft availed.
   (Other Love— Ah, my One, forgive!—)
To aid, when Churus and Opium failed;—
   I could not suffer so much and live.
      Ahi, Yasmini, who had to live!

Nay, why should I say "Forgive" to Thee?
   To whom my lovers and I are naught,
Who granted some passionate nights to me,
   Then rose and left me with never a thought!
And yet, ah, yet, for those Nights that Were,
   Thy passive limbs and thy loose loved hair,
I would pay, as I *have* paid, all these days,
   With the love that kills and the thought that slays
      Ahi, Yasmini, thy youth it slays!

The youthful widow, with shaven hair,
   Whose senses ache for the love of a man,
The young Priest, knowing that women are fair,
   Who stems his longing as best he can,
These suffer not as I suffer for Thee;
   For the Soul desires what the senses crave,
There will never be pleasure or peace for me,

Since He who wounded, alone could save.
Ahi, Yasmini, He will not save!

The torchlight flares, and the lovers lean
  Towards Yasmini, with yearning eyes,
Who dances, wondering what they mean,
  And gives cold kisses, and scant replies.
They talk of Love, she withholds the name,—
  (Love came to her as a Flame of Fire!)
From things that are only a weary shame;
  Trivial Vanity;—light Desire.
    Ahi, Yasmini, the light Desire!

Yasmini bends to the praise of men,
  And looks in the mirror, upon her hand,[1]
To curse the beauty that failed her then—
  Ah, none of her lovers can understand!
How her whole life hung on that beauty's **power**,
  The spell that waned at the final test,
The charm that paled in the vital hour,—
  Which won so many,—yet lost the best!
    Ahi, Yasmini, who lost the best!

She leaves the dancing to reach the roof,
  With the lover who claims the passing **hour**,
Her lips are his, but her eyes aloof
  While the starlight falls in a silver shower.

[1] Indian women wear a small mirror in a ring on their thumbs.

Let him take what pleasure, what love, he may,
He, too, will suffer ere life be spent,—
But Yasmini's soul has wandered away
 To join the Lover, who came,—and went!
  Ahi, Yasmini, He came,—and went!

## Among the Rice Fields

She was fair as a Passion-flower,
   (But little of love he knew.)
Her lucent eyes were like amber wine,
   And her eyelids stained with blue.

He called them the Gates of Fair Desire,
   And the Lakes where Beauty lay,
But I looked into them once, and saw
   The eyes of Beasts of Prey.

He praised her teeth, that were small and white
   As lilies upon his lawn,
While I remembered a tiger's fangs
   That met in a speckled fawn.

She had her way; a lover the more,
   And I had a friend the less.
For long there was nothing to do but wait
   And suffer his happiness.

But now I shall choose the sharpest Kriss
   And nestle it in her breast,
For dead, he is drifting down to sea,
   And his own hand wrought his rest.

## The Bride

Beat on the Tom-toms, and scatter the flowers,
    Jasmine, Hibiscus, vermilion and white,
This is the day, and the Hour of Hours,
    Bring forth the Bride for her Lover's delight.
Maidens no more, as a maiden shall claim her,
    Near, in his Mystery, draweth Desire.
Who, if she waver a moment, shall blame her?
    She is a flower, and love is a fire.
            Choti Tinchaurya syani hogayi! [1]


Give her the anklets, the rings and the necklace,
    Darken her eyelids with delicate Art,
Heighten the beauty, so youthful and fleckless,
    By the Gods favoured, oh, Bridegroom thou art!
Twine in thy fingers her fingers so slender,
    Circle together the Mystical Fire,
Bridegroom,—a whisper—be gentle and tender,
    Choti Tinchaurya knows not desire.
            Abhi Tinchaurya syani hogayi!

[1] *Anglice:* Little Tinchaurya has grown up.

Bring forth the silks and the veil that shall cover
    Beauty, till yesterday, careless and wild,
Red are her lips for the kiss of a lover,
    Ripe are her breasts for the lips of a child.
Centre and Shrine of Mysterious Power,
    Chalice of Pleasure and Rose of Delight,
Shyly aware of the swift-coming hour,
    Waiting the shade and the silence of night,
              Choti Tinchaurya syani hogayi!

Still must the Bridegroom his longing dissemble,
    Longing to loosen the silk-woven cord,
Ah, how his fingers will flutter and tremble,
    Fingers well skilled with the bridle and sword.
Thine is his valour, oh, Bride, and his beauty,
    Thine to possess and re-issue again,
Such is thy tender and passionate duty,
    Licit thy pleasure and honoured thy pain.
              Choti Tinchaurya syani hogayi!

Choti Tinchaurya, lovely and tender,
    Still all unbroken to sorrow and strife.
Come to the Bridegroom who, silk-clad and slender
    Brings thee the Honour and Burden of Life.
Bidding farewell to thy light-hearted playtime,
    Worship thy Lover with fear and delight,
Art thou not ever, though slave of his daytime,
    Choti Tinchaurya, queen of his night?
              Choti Tinchaurya syani hogayi!

# *Unanswered*

Something compels me, somewhere. Yet I see
No clear command in Life's long mystery.

Oft have I flung myself beside my horse,
   To drink the water from the roadside mire,
And felt the liquid through my being course,
   Stilling the anguish of my thirst's desire.

A simple want; so easily allayed;
After the burning march; water and shade.

Also I lay against the loved one's heart
   Finding fulfilment in that resting-place,
Feeling my longing, quenched, was but a part
   Of nature's ceaseless striving for the race.

But now, I know not what they would with me
Matter or Force or God, if Gods there be.

I wait; I question; Nature heeds me not.
   She does but urge in answer to my prayer,
"Arise and do!" Alas, she adds not what;
   "Arise and go!" Alas, she says not where!

# The Net of Memory

I cast the Net of Memory,
Man's torment and delight,
Over the level Sands of Youth
That lay serenely bright,
Their tranquil gold at times submerged
In the Spring Tides of Love's Delight.

The Net brought up, in silver gleams,
Forgotten truth and fancies fair:
Like opal shells, small happy facts
Within the Net entangled were
With the red coral of his lips,
The waving seaweed of his hair.

We were so young; he was so fair.

# The Cactus Thicket

"The Atlas summits were veiled in purple gloom,
    But a golden moon above rose clear and free.
The cactus thicket was ruddy with scarlet bloom
    Where, through the silent shadow, he came to me

"All my sixteen summers were but for this,
    That He should pass, and, pausing, find me fair.
You Stars! bear golden witness! My lips were his;
    I would not live till others have fastened there."

"Oh, take me, Death, ere ever the charm shall fade,
    Ah, close these eyes, ere ever the dream grow dim.
I welcome thee with rapture, and unafraid,
    Even as yesternight I welcomed Him."

    \*    \*    \*    \*    \*    \*

"Not now, Impatient one; it well may be
That ten moons hence I shall return for thee."

## Song of the Peri

Beauty, the Gift of Gifts, I give to thee.
    Pleasure and love shall spring around thy feet
As through the lake the lotuses arise
    Pinkly transparent and divinely sweet.

I give thee eyes aglow like morning stars,
    Delicate brows, a mist of sable tresses,
That all the journey of thy life may be
    Lit up by love and softened by caresses.

For those who once were proud and softly bred
    Shall, kneeling, wait thee as thou passest by,
They who were pure shall stretch forth eager hands
    Crying, "Thy pity, Lord, before we die!"

And one shall murmur, "If the sun at dawn
    Shall open and caress a happy flower,
What blame to him, although the blossom fade
    In the full splendour of his noontide power?"

And one, "If aloes close together grow
    It well may chance a plant shall wounded be,

Pierced by the thorntips of another's leaves,
   Thus am I hurt unconsciously by thee."

For some shall die and many more shall sin,
   Suffering for thy sake till seven times seven,
Because of those most perfect lips of thine
   Which held the power to make or mar their heaven

And though thou givest back but cruelty,
   Their love, persistent, shall not heed nor care,
All those whose ears are fed with blame of thee
   Shall say, "It may be so, but he was fair."

Ay, those who lost the whole of youth for thee,
   Made early and for ever, shamed and sad,
Shall sigh, re-living some sweet memory,
   "Ah, once it was his will to make me glad."

Thy nights shall be as bright as summer days,
   The sequence of thy sins shall seem as duty,
Since I have given thee, oh, Gift of Gifts!—
   The pale perfection of unrivalled beauty.

# Though in My Firmament Thou Wilt Not Shine

TALK not, my Lord, of unrequited love,
   Since love requites itself most royally.
Do we not live but by the sun above,
   And takes he any heed of thee or me?

Though in my firmament thou wilt not shine,
   Thy glory, as a Star, is none the less.
Oh, Rose, though all unplucked by hand of mine
   Still am I debtor to thy loveliness.

## The Convert

The sun was hot on the tamarind trees,
   Their shadows shrivelled and shrank.
No coolness came on the off-shore breeze
   That rattled the scrub on the bank.
She stretched her appealing arms to me,
Uplifting the Flagon of Love to me,
Till—great indeed was my unslaked thirst—
   I paused, I stooped, and I drank!

I went with my foe to the edge of the crater,—
   But one to return, we knew,—
The lava's heat had never been greater
   Than the ire between us two.
He flung back his head and he mocked at me,
He spat unspeakable words at me,
Our eyes met, and our knives met,
   I saw red, and I slew!

Such were my deeds when my youth was hot,
   And force was new to my hand,
With many more that I tell thee not,
   Well known in my native land.

These show thy Christ when thou prayest to Him
He too was a man thou sayest of Him,
Therefore He, when I reach His feet,
  Will remember, and understand.

## Ashore

O<small>UT</small> I came from the dancing-place:
The night-wind met me face to face—

A wind off the harbour, cold and keen,
"I know," it whistled, "where thou hast been.

A faint voice fell from the stars above—
"Thou? whom we lighted to shrines of Love!

I found when I reached my lonely room
A faint sweet scent in the unlit gloom.

And this was the worst of all to bear,
For someone had left white lilac there.

The flower you loved, in times that were.

## Yasin Khan

Ay, thou hast found thy kingdom, Yasin Khan,
   Thy fathers' pomp and power are thine, at last.
No more the rugged roads of Khorasan,
   The scanty food and tentage of the past!

Wouldst thou make war? thy followers know no fear,
   Where shouldst thou lead them but to victory?
Wouldst thou have love? thy soft-eyed slaves draw near
   Eager to drain thy strength away from thee.

My thoughts drag backwards to forgotten days,
   To scenes etched deeply on my heart by pain;
The thirsty marches, ambuscades, and frays,
   The hostile hills, the burnt and barren plain.

Hast thou forgotten how one night was spent,
   Crouched in a camel's carcase by the road,
Along which Akbar's soldiers, scouting, went,
   And he himself, all unsuspecting, rode.

Did we not waken one despairing dawn,
   Attacked in front, cut off in rear, by snow.

Till, like a tiger leaping on a fawn,
   Half of the hill crashed down upon the foe?

Once, as thou mournd'st thy lifeless brother's fate,
   The red tears falling from thy shattered wrist,
A spent Waziri, forceful still, in hate,
   Covered thy heart, ten paces off,—and missed!

Ahi, men thrust a worn and dinted sword
   Into a velvet-scabbarded repose;
The gilded pageants that salute thee Lord
   Cover *one* sorrow-rusted heart, God knows.

Ah, to exchange this wealth of idle days
   For one cold reckless night of Khorasan!
To crouch once more before the camp-fire blaze
   That lit the lonely eyes of Yasin Khan.

To watch the starlight glitter on the snows,
   The plain stretched round us like a waveless sea,
Waiting until thy weary lids should close
   To slip my furs and spread them over thee.

How the wind howled about the lonely pass,
   While the faint snowshine of that plateau'd space
Lit, where it lay upon the frozen grass,
   The mournful, tragic beauty of thy face.

Thou hast enough caressed the scented hair
    Of these soft-breasted girls who waste thee so;
Hast thou not sons for every adult year?
    Let us arise, O Yasin Khan, and go!

Let us escape from out these prison bars
    To gain the freedom of an open sky,
Thy soul and mine, alone beneath the stars,
    Intriguing danger, as in days gone by.

Nay; there is no returning, Yasin Khan.
    The white peaks ward the passes, as of yore,
The wind sweeps o'er the wastes of Khorasan;—
    But thou and I go thitherward no more.

Close, ah, too close, the bitter knowledge clings
    We may not follow where my fancies yearn
The years go hence, and wild and lovely things
    *Their own,* go with them, never to return.

## Khristna and His Flute
(Translation by Moolchand)

Be still, my heart, and listen,
   For sweet and yet acute
I hear the wistful music
   Of Khristna and his flute.
Across the cool, blue evenings,
   Throughout the burning days,
Persuasive and beguiling,
   He plays and plays and plays.

Ah, none may hear such music
   Resistant to its charms,
The household work grows weary,
   And cold the husband's arms.
I must arise and follow,
   To seek, in vain pursuit,
The blueness and the distance,
   The sweetness of that flute!

In linked and liquid sequence,
   The plaintive notes dissolve

Divinely tender secrets
    That none but he can solve.
Oh, Khristna, I am coming,
    I can no more delay.
"My heart has flown to join thee,"
    How shall my footsteps stay?

Beloved, such thoughts have peril;
    The wish is in my mind
That I had fired the jungle,
    And left no leaf behind,—
Burnt all bamboos to ashes,
    And made their music mute,—
To save thee from the magic
    Of Khristna and his flute.

## Song of Jasoda

Had I been young I could have claimed to fold thee
   For many days against my eager breast;
But, as things are, how can I hope to hold thee
   Once thou hast wakened from this fleeting rest?

Clear shone the moonlight, so that thou couldst find me
   Yet not so clear that thou couldst see my face,
Where in the shadow of the palms behind me
   I waited for thy steps, for thy embrace.

What reck I now my morning life was lonely?
   For widowed feet the ways are always rough.
Though thou hast come to me at sunset only,
   Still thou hast come, my Lord, it is enough.

Ah, mine no more the glow of dawning beauty,
   The fragrance and the dainty gloss of youth,
Worn by long years of solitude and duty,
   I have no bloom to offer thee in truth.

Yet, since these eyes of mine have never wandered,
   Still may they gleam with long forgotten light.

Since in no wanton way my youth was squandered,
　　Some sense of youth still clings to me to-night.

*Thy* lips are fresh as dew on budding roses,
　　The gold of dawn still lingers in thy hair,
While the abandonment of sleep discloses
　　How every attitude of youth is fair.

Thou art so pale, I hardly dare caress thee,
　　Too brown my fingers show against the white.
Ahi, the glory, that I should possess thee,
　　Ahi, the grief, but for a single night!

The tulip tree has pallid golden flowers
　　That grow more rosy as their petals fade;
Such is the splendour of my evening hours
　　Whose time of youth was wasted in the shade.

I shall not wait to see to-morrow's morning,
　　Too bright the golden dawn for me,—too bright,—
How could I bear thine eyes' unconscious scorning
　　Of what so pleased thee in the dimmer light?

It may be wine had brought some brief illusion,
　　Filling thy brain with rainbow fantasy,
Or youth, with moonlight, making sweet collusion,
　　Threw an alluring glamour over me.

Therefore I leave thee softly, to awaken
   When the first sun rays warm thy blue-veined breast
Smiling and all unknowing I have taken
   The poppied drink that brings me endless rest.

Thus would I have thee rise; thy fancy laden
   With the vague sweetness of the bygone night,
Thinking of me as some consenting maiden,
   Whose beauty blossomed first for thy delight.

While I, if any kindly visions hover
   Around the silence of my last repose,
Shall dream of thee, my pale and radiant lover,
   Who made my life so lovely at its close!

## Song of Ramesram Temple Girl

Now is the season of my youth,
   Not thus shall I always be,
Listen, dear Lord, thou too art young,
   Take thy pleasure with me.
My hair is straight as the falling rain,
   And fine as the morning mist,
I am a rose awaiting thee
   That none have touched or kissed.

      Do as thou wilt with mine and me
        Beloved, I only pray,
      Follow the promptings of thy youth,
        Let there be no delay!

A leaf that flutters upon the bough,
   A moment, and it is gone,—
A bubble amid the fountain spray,—
   Ah, pause, and think thereon;
For such is youth and its passing bloom
   That wait for thee this hour,
If aught in thy heart incline to me
   Ah, stoop and pluck thy flower!

    Come, my Lord, to the temple shade
     Where cooling fountains play,
    If aught in thy heart incline to love
     Let there be no delay!

Many shall faint with love of me
 And I shall slake their thirst,
But Fate has brought thee hither to-day
 That thou shouldst be the first.
Old, so old are the temple-walls,
 Love is older than they;
But I am the short-lived temple rose,
 Blooming for thee to-day.

    Thine am I, Prince, and only thine,
     What is there more to say?
    If aught in thy heart incline to love
     Let there be no delay!

## The Rao of Ilore

I was sold to the Rao of Ilore,
   Slender and tall was he.
When his litter carried him down the street
   I peeped through the thatch to see.
        Ah, the eyes of the Rao of Ilore
        My lover that was to be!

The hair that lay on his youthful brow
   Was curled like an ocean wave;
His eyes were lit with a tender smile,
   But his lips were soft and grave.
For sake of these things I was still with joy
   When the silver coins were paid,
And they took me up to the Palace gates,
   Delighted and unafraid.
        Ah, the eyes of the Rao of Ilore,
        May never their brilliance fade!

So near was I to the crown of life!
   Ten thousand times, alas!
The Diwan leant from the latticed hall,
   Looked down and saw me pass.

He begged for me from the Rao of Ilore,
 Who answered, "She is thine,
Thou wert ever more than a father to me,
 And thy desires are mine."
   Ah, the eyes of the Rao of Ilore
   That never had looked in mine!

My years were spent in the Diwan's Courts,
 My youth died down that day.
For sake of thine own content of mind
 My lost beloved, I pray
That never my Lord a love may know
 Like that he threw away.
   Ah, the eyes of the Rao of Ilore,
   Who threw my life away!

## To M. C. N.

Thou hast no wealth, nor any pride of power,
    Thy life is offered on affection's altar.
Small sacrifices claim thee, hour by hour,
    Yet on the tedious path thou dost not falter.

To the unknowing, well thy days might seem
    Circled by solitude and tireless duty,
Yet is thy soul made radiant by a dream
    Of delicate and rainbow-coloured beauty.

Never a flower trembles in the wind,
    Never a sunset lingers on the sea,
But something of its fragrance joins thy mind,
    Some sparkle of its light remains with thee.

Thus when thy spirit enters on its rest,
Thy lips shall say, "I too have known the best!

## Disappointment

Oh, come, Beloved, before my beauty fades,
   Pity the sorrow of my loneliness.
I am a Rosebush that the Cypress shades,
   No sunbeams find or lighten my distress.

Daily I watch the waning of my bloom.
   Ah, piteous fading of a thing so fair!
While Fate, remorseless, weaving at her loom,
   Twines furtive silver in my twisted hair.

This noon I watched a tremulous fading rose
   Rise on the wind to court a butterfly.
"One speck of pollen, ere my petals close,
   Bring me one touch of love before I die!"

But the gay butterfly, who had the power
   To grant, refused, flew far across the dell,
And, as he fertilised a younger flower,
   The petals of the rose, defrauded, fell.

Such was my fate, thou hast not come to me,
   Thine eyes are absent, and thy voice is mute

Though I am slim, as this Papaya tree,
  With breasts out-pointing, even as its fruit.

Beauty was mine, it brought me no caress,
  My lips were red, yet there were none to taste,
I saw my youth consume in loneliness,
  And all the fervour of my heart run waste.

While I still hoped that Thou wouldst come to me,
  I and the garden waited for their Lord.
Here He will rest, beneath this Champa tree;
  Hence, all ye spike-set grasses from the sward!

In this cool rillet I shall bathe His feet,
  Come, rounded pebbles from a smoother shore.
This is the honey that His lips will eat,
  Hasten, O bees, enhance the amber store!

Ripen, ye Custard Apples, round and fair,
  Practice your songs, O Bulbuls, on the bough,
Surely some sweeter sweetness haunts the air;
  Maybe His feet draw near us, even now!

Disperse, ye fireflies, clustered on the palm,
  Love heeds no lamp, he welcomes moonless skies
Soon shall ye find, O stars, serene and calm,
  Your sparkling rivals in my lover's eyes!

Closely I wove my leafy Jasmine bowers,
  Hoping to hide my pleasure and my shame,

Where the Lantana's indecisive flowers
  Vary from palest rose to orange flame.

Ay, there were lovely hours, 'neath fern and palm
  Almost my aching longing I forgot.
White nights of silence, noons of golden calm,
  All past, all wasted, since Thou camest not!

Night after night the Champa trees distilled
  Their cruel sweetness on the careless air.
Noon after noon I watched the Bulbuls build,
  And saw with hungry eyes the Sun-birds pair.

None came, and none will come; no use to wait,—
  Youth's fragrance dies, its tender light dies down
I will arise, before it grows too late,
  And seek the noisy brilliance of the town.

These many waiting years I longed for gold,
  Now must I needs console me with alloy.
Before this beauty fades, this pulse grows cold,
  I may not love, I will at least enjoy!

Farewell, my Solitude of scented flowers,
  Across whose glades the emerald parrots gleam,
Haunt of false hope, and home of wasted hours,
  I am awake, at last,—Guard thou the dream!

## On Pilgrimage

Oh, youthful bearer of my palanquin,
   Thy glossy hair lies loosened on thy neck,
The "tears of labour" gem thy velvet skin,
   Whose even texture knows no other fleck.

Thy slender shoulder strains beneath my weight;
   Too fair thou art for work, sweet slave of mine
Would that this idle breast, reversing fate,
   A willing serf to love, supported thine!

I smell the savage scent of sun-warmed fur
   Close in the Jungle, musky, hot and sweet.—
The air comes from thy shoulder, even as myrrh,
   Would we were as the panthers, free to meet.

The Temple road is steep; I grieve to see
   Thy slender ankles bruised among the clods.
Oh, my Beloved, if I might worship thee!
   Beauty is greater far than all the Gods.

## The Rice-Boat

I slept upon the Rice-boat
    That, reef protected, lay
At anchor, where the palm-trees
    Infringe upon the bay.
The windless air was heavy
    With cinnamon and rose,
The midnight calm seemed waiting
    Too fateful for repose.

One joined me on the Rice-boat
    With wild and waving hair,
Whose vivid words and laughter
    Awoke the silent air.
Oh, beauty, bare and shining,
    Fresh washen in the bay,
One well may love by moonlight
    What one would not love by day!

Above among the cordage
    The night wind hardly stirred,
The lapping of the ripples
    Was all the sound we heard.

Love reigned upon the Rice-boat,
  And Peace controlled the sea,
The spirit's consolation,
  The senses' ecstasy.

Though many things and mighty
  Are furthered in the West,
The ancient Peace has vanished
  Before To-day's unrest.
For how among their striving,
  Their gold, their lust, their drink,
Shall men find time for dreaming
  Or any space to think?

Think not I scorn the Science
  That lightens human pain;
Though man's reliance often
  Is placed on it in vain.
Maybe the long endeavour,
  The patience and the strife,
May some day solve the riddle,
  The Mystery of Life.

Perchance I do not value
  Things Western as I ought,
The trains,—that take us, whither?
  The ships,—that reach, what port?
To me it seems but chaos
  Of greed and haste and rage,

The endless, aimless, motion
  Of squirrels in a cage.

Here, where some ruined temple
  In solitude decays,
With carven walls still hallowed
  With prayers of bygone days,
Here, where the coral outcrops
  Make "flowers of the sea,"
The olden Peace yet lingers,
  In hushed serenity.

Ah, silent, silver moonlight,
  Whose charm impartial falls
On tanks of sacred water
  And squalid city walls,
Whose mystic whiteness hallows
  The lowest and the least,
To thee men owe the glamour
  That draws them to the East.

And as this azure water,
  Unflecked by wave or foam,
Conceals in its tranquillity
  The dreaded white shark's home
So if love be illusion
  I ask the dream to stay,
Content to love by moonlight
  What I might not love by day.

## Lallji, My Desire

"This is no time for saying 'no'"
   Were thy last words to me,
And yet my lips refused the kiss
   They might have given thee.
         How could I know
         That thou wouldst go
         To sleep so far from me?

They took thee to the Burning-Ghat,
   Oh, Lallji, my desire.
And now a faint and lonely flame
   Uprises from the pyre.
The thin grey smoke in spirals drifts
   Across the opal sky.
Would that I were a wife of thine,
   And thus with thee could die!
         How could I know
         That thou wouldst go,
         Oh, Lallji, my desire?
         The lips I missed
         The flames have kissed
         Upon the Sandal pyre.

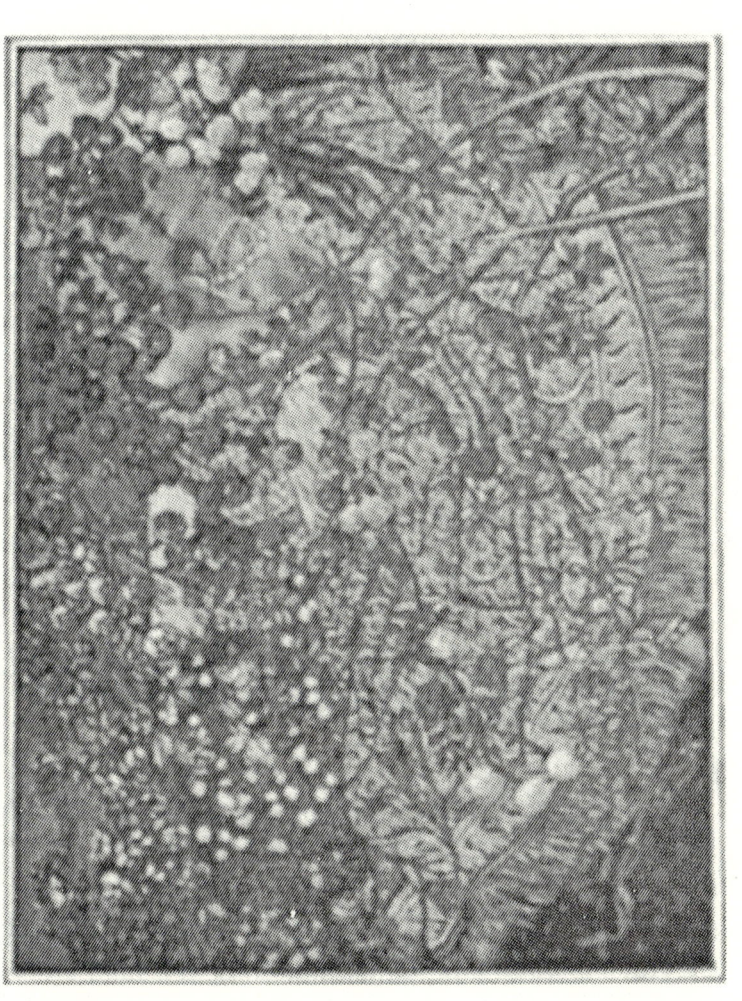

Lallji, My Desire

If one should meet me with a knife
   And cut my heart in twain,
Then would he see the smoke arise
   From every severed vein.
Such is the burning, inward fire,
   The anguish of my pain,
For my Beloved, whose dying lips
   Implored a kiss—in vain!
          How could I know
          That thou wouldst go,
          Oh, Lallji, my desire?
          Too young thou art
          To lay thy heart
          Upon the Sandal pyre.

Thy wife awaits her coming child;
   What were a child to me,
If I might take thee in these arms
   And face the flames with thee?
The priests are chanting round the pyre
   At dusk they will depart
And leave to thee thy lonely rest,
   To me my lonelier heart.
          How could I know
          Thou lovedst me so?
          Upon the Sandal pyre
          He lies forsaken.
          The flames have taken
          My Lallji, my desire!

## Rutland Gate

His back is bent and his lips are blue,
    Shivering out in the wet:
"Here's a florin, my man, for you,
    Go and get drunk and forget!"

Right in the midst of a Christian land,
    Rotted with wealth and ease,
Broken and dragged they let him stand
    Till his feet on the pavement freeze.

God leaves His poor in His vicars' care,
    For He hears the church-bells ring,
His ears are buzzing with constant prayer
    And the hymns His people sing.

Can His pity picture the anguish here,
    Can He see, through a London fog,
The man who has worked "nigh seventy year"
    To die the death of a dog?

No one heeds him, the crowds pass on.
    Why does he want to live?
"Take this florin, and get you gone,
    Go and get drunk,—and forgive!"

## *Atavism*

Deep in the jungle vast and dim,
   That knew not a white man's feet,
I smelt the odour of sun-warmed fur,
   Musky, savage and sweet.

Far it was from the huts of men
   And the grass where Sambur feed;
I threw a stone at a Kadapu tree
   That bled as a man might bleed.

Scent of fur and colour of blood:—
   And the long dead instincts rose,
I followed the lure of my season's mate,—
   And flew, bare-fanged, at my foes.

\*    \*    \*

Pale days: and a league of laws
   Made by the whims of men.
Would I were back with my furry cubs
   In the dusk of a jungle den.

## Middle-Age

The sins of Youth are hardly sins,
   So frank they are and free.
'T is but when Middle-age begins
   We need morality.

Ah, pause and weigh this bitter truth:
   That Middle-age, grown cold,
No comprehension has of Youth,
   No pity for the Old.

Youth, with his half-divine mistakes,
   She never can forgive,
So much she hates his charm which makes
   Worth while the life we live.

She scorns Old Age, whose tolerance
   And calm, well-balanced mind
(Knowing how crime is born of chance)
   Can pardon all mankind.

Yet she, alas! has all the power
   Of strength and place and gold,

Man's every act, through every hour,
   Is by her laws controlled.

All things she grasps with sordid hands
   And weighs in tarnished scales.
She neither feels, nor understands,
   And yet her will prevails!

Cold-blooded vice and careful sin,
   Gold-lust, blind selfishness,—
The shortest, cheapest way to win
   Some, worse than cheap, success.

Such are her attributes and aims,
   Yet meekly we obey,
While she to guide and order claims
   All issues of the day.

You seek for honour, friendship, truth?
   Let Middle-age be banned!
Go, for warm-hearted acts, to Youth;
   To Age,—to understand!

## The Jungle Flower

Ah, the cool silence of the shaded hours,
The scent and colour of the jungle flowers!

Thou are one of the jungle flowers, strange and fierce and fair,
  Palest amber, perfect lines, and scented with champa flower.
Lie back and frame thy face in the gloom of thy loosened hair;
  Sweet thou art and loved—ay, loved—for an hour.

But thought flies far, ah, far, to another breast,
  Whose whiteness breaks to the rose of a twin pink flower,
Where wind the azure veins that my lips caressed
  When Fate was gentle to me for a too-brief hour.

There is my spirit's home and my soul's abode,
The rest are only inns on the traveller's road.

## From Behind the Lattice

I SEE your red-golden hair and know
   How white the hidden skin must be,
Though sun-kissed face and fingers show
The fervour of the noon-day glow,
   The keenness of the sea.

My longing fancies ebb and flow,
   Still circling constant unto this;
My great desire (ah, whisper low)
To plant on thy forbidden snow
   The rosebud of a kiss.

The scarlet flower would spread and grow,
   Your whiteness change and flush,
(Be still, my reckless heart, beat slow,
'T is but a dream that stirs thee so!)
   To one transparent blush.

## *Wings*

Was it worth while to forego our wings
    To gain these dextrous hands?
Truly they fashion us wonderful things
    As the fancy of man demands.

But—to fly! to sail through the lucid air
    From crest to violet crest
Of these great grey mountains, quartz-veined and bare
    Where the white clouds gather and rest.

Even to flutter from flower to flower,—
    To skim the tops of the trees,—
In the roseate light of a sun-setting hour
    To drift on a sea-going breeze.

Ay, the hands have marvellous skill
    To create us curious things,—
Baubles, playthings, weapons to kill,—
    But—I would we had chosen wings!

# Song of the Parao (Camping-Ground)

Heart, my heart, thou hast found thy home!
   From gloom and sorrow thou hast come forth,
Thou who wast foolish, and sought to roam
   'Neath the cruel stars of the frozen North.

Thou hast returned to thy dear delights;
   The golden glow of the quivering days,
The silver silence of tropical nights,
   No more to wander in alien ways.

      Here, each star is a well-loved friend;
      To me and my heart at the journey's end.

These are my people, and this my land,
   I hear the pulse of her secret soul.
This is the life that I understand,
   Savage and simple and sane and whole.

      Washed in the light of a clear fierce sun,—
      Heart, my heart, the journey is done.

See! the painted piece of the skies,
Where the rose-hued opal of sunset lies.

    Hear the passionate Koel calling
    From coral trees, where the dusk is falling.
See my people, slight limbed and tall.
    The maiden's bosom they scorn to cover:
The breasts that shall call and enthral her lover,
    Things of beauty, are free to all.

Free to the eyes, that think no shame
    That a girl should bloom like a forest flower.
Who hold that Love is a sacred flame,—
    Outward beauty a God-like dower.

Who further regard it as no disgrace
If loveliness lessen to serve the race,
Nor point the finger of jesting scorn
At her who carries the child unborn.

        Ah, my heart, but we wandered far
        From the light of the slanting fourfold Star!

Oh, palm-leaf thatch, where the melon thrives
Beneath the shade of the tamarind tree,
Thou coverest tranquil, graceful lives,
That want so little, that knew no haste,
    Nor the bitter goad of a too-full hour;
Whose soft-eyed women are lithe and tall,
And wear no garment below the knee,
    Nor veil or raiment above the waist,

But the beautiful hair, that dowers them all,
  And falls to the ground in a scented shower.

The youths return from their swift-flowing bath,
  With the swinging grace that their height allows,
Lightly climbing the river-side path,
  Their soft hair knotted above their brows.
Elephants wade the darkening river,
  Their bells, which tinkle in minor thirds,
Faintly sweet, like passionate birds
  Whose warbling wakens a sense of pain,—
Thrill through the nerves and make them quiver,
  Heart, my heart, art thou happy again?

Here is beauty to feast thine eyes.
  Here is the land of thy long desire.
See how the delicate spirals rise
  Azure and faint from the wood-fed fire.

Where the cartmen wearily share their food,
  Ere they, by their bullocks, lie down to rest,
Heart of mine, dost thou find it good,
  This wide red road by the winds caressed?

    This lone Parao, where the fireflies light?
    These tom-toms, fretting the peace of night?

Heart, thou hast wandered and suffered much,
  Death has robbed thee, and Life betrayed,

But there is ever a solace for such
   In that they are not lightly afraid.

The strength that found them the fire to love
   Finds them also the force to forget.
Thy joy in thy dreaming lives to prove
   Thou art not mortally wounded yet.

Here, 'neath the arch of the vast, clear sky,
   Where range upon range the remote grey hills
Far in the distance recede and die,
   There is no space for thy trivial ills.

On the low horizon towards the sea,
   Faint yet vivid, the lightnings play,
The lucid air is kind as a kiss,
   The falling twilight is cool and grey.
        What has sorrow to do with thee?
        Love was cruel? Thou now art free.
        Life unkind? It has given thee this!

## The Tom-Toms

Dost thou hear the tom-toms throbbing,
Like a lonely lover sobbing
For the beauty that is robbing him of all his life's delight?
Plaintive sounds, restrained, enthralling,
Seeking through the twilight falling
Something lost beyond recalling, in the darkness of the
                                                                         night.

Oh, my little, loved Firoza,
Come and nestle to me closer,
Where the golden-balled Mimosa makes a canopy above,
For the day, so hot and burning,
Dies away, and night, returning,
Sets thy lover's spirit yearning for thy beauty and thy love.

Soon will come the rosy warning
Of the bright relentless morning,
When, thy soft caresses scorning, I shall leave thee in the
                                                                          shade.
All the day my work must chain me,
And its weary bonds restrain me,
For I may not re-attain thee till the light begins to fade.

But at length the long day endeth,
As the cool of night descendeth
His last strength thy lover spendeth in returning to thy breast,
Where beneath the Babul nightly,
While the planets shimmer whitely,
And the fire-flies glimmer brightly, thou shalt give him love and rest.

Far away, across the distance,
The quick-throbbing drums' persistence
Shall resound, with soft insistence, in the pauses of delight,
Through the sequence of the hours,
While the starlight and the flowers
Consecrate this love of ours, in the Temple of the Night.

# *Written in Cananore*

## I

Who was it held that Love was soothing or sweet?
Mine is a painful fire, at its whitest heat.

Who said that Beauty was ever a gentle joy?
Thine is a sword that flashes but to destroy.

Though mine eyes rose up from thy Beauty's banquet, calm
                                        and refreshed,
My lips, that were granted naught, can find no rest.

My soul was linked with thine, through speech and silent
                                            hours,
As the sound of two soft flutes combined, or the scent of
                                            sister flowers.

But the body, that wretched slave of the Sultan, Mind,
Who follows his master ever, but far behind,

Nothing was granted him, and every rebellious cell
Rises up with angry protest, "It is not well!
Night is falling; thou hast departed; I am alone;

And the Last Sweetness of Love thou hast not given—I have
not known!"

## II

Somewhere, oh, My Beloved One, the house is standing,
Waiting for thee and me; for our first caresses.
It may be a river-boat, or a wave-washed landing,
The shade of a tree in the jungle's dim recesses,
      Some far-off mountain tent, ill-pitched and lonely,
      Or the naked vault of the purple heavens only.

But the Place is waiting there; till the Hour shall show it,
And our footsteps, following Fate, find it and know it.

Where we shall worship the greatest of all the Gods in his
pomp and power,—
I sometimes think that I shall not care to survive that hour!

# Feroke

The rice-birds fly so white, so silver white,
    The velvet rice-flats lie so emerald green,
My heart inhales, with sorrowful delight,
    The sweet and poignant sadness of the scene.

The swollen tawny river seeks the sea,
    Its hungry waters, never satisfied,
Beflecked with fallen log and torn-up tree,
    Engulf the fisher-huts on either side.

The current brought a stranger yesterday,
    And laid him on the sand beneath a palm,
His worn young face was partly torn away,
    His eyes, that saw the world no more, were calm.

We could not close his eyelids, stiff with blood,—
    But, oh, my brother, I had changed with thee!
For I am still tormented in the flood,
    Whilst thou hast done thy work, and reached the sea

## My Desire

Fate has given me many a gift
   To which men most aspire,
Lovely, precious and costly things,
   But not my heart's desire.

Many a man has a secret dream
   Of where his soul would be.
Mine is a low verandah'd house
   In a tope beside the sea.

Over the roof tall palms should wave,
   Swaying from side to side,
Every night we should fall asleep
   To the rhythm of the tide.

The dawn should be gay with song of birds,
   And the stir of fluttering wings.
Surely the joy of life is hid
   In simple and tender things!

At eve the waves would shimmer with gold
   In the rosy sunset rays,

Emerald velvet flats of rice
  Would rest the landward gaze.

A boat must rock at the laterite steps
  In a reef-protected pool,
For we should sail through the starlit night
  When the winds were calm and cool.

I am so tired of all this world,
  Its folly and fret and care.
Find me a little scented home
  Amongst thy loosened hair.

Give me a soft and secret place
  Against thine amber breast,
Where, hidden away from all mankind,
  My soul may come to rest.

Many a man has a secret dream
  Of where his life might be;
Mine is a lovely, lonely place
  With sunshine and the sea.

## Sher Afzul

This was the tale Sher Afzul told to me,
   While the spent camels bubbled on their knees,
And ruddy camp-fires twinkled through the gloom
   Sweet with the fragrance from the Sinjib trees.

I had a friend who lay, condemned to death
   In gaol for murder, wholly innocent,
Yet caught in webs of luckless circumstance;—
   Thou know'st how lies, of good and ill intent,

Cluster like flies around a justice-court,
   Wheel within wheel, revolving screw on screw;—
But from his prison he escaped and fled,
   Keeping his liberty a night or two

Among the lonely hills, where, shackled still,
   He braved a village, seeking for a file
To loose his irons; alas! he lost his life
   Through the base sweetness of a woman's smile.

Lovely she was, and young, who gave the youth
   Kind words, and promised succor and repose,

Till on the quilt of false security
    He found exhausted sleep; but, ere he rose,

Entered the guards, brought by her messenger.
    Thus was he captured, slain, and on her breast
Soon shone the guerdon of her treachery,
    The price of blood; in gold made manifest.

I might have killed her? Brave men have died thus.
    Revenge demanded keener punishment.
So I walked softly on those lilac hills,
    Touching my *rhibab* lightly as I went.

I found her fair: 'twas no unpleasant task
    In the young spring-time when the fruit-trees flower
To pass her door, and pause, and pass again,
    Shading mine eyes against her beauty's power.

Warmly I wooed her, while the almond trees
    Broke into fragile clouds of rosy snow.
Her dawning passion feared her lord's return,
    Ever she pleaded softly, "Let us go."

But I spoke tenderly, and said, "Beloved,
    Shall not thy lips give orders to my heart?
Yet there is one small matter in these hills
    Claiming attention ere I can depart.

"Let us not waste these days; thine absent lord
    Cannot return, thou know'st, before the snow

Has melted, and the almond fruits appear."
  This time she answered, "Naught but thee I know!"

I too was young; I could have loved her well
  When her soft eyes across the twilight burned;
But suddenly, around her amber neck,
  The golden beads would sparkle as she turned.

*And I remembered;* swift mine eyelids fell
  To hide the hate that festered in my soul,
Ever more deeply, with the rising fear
  That Love might wrench Revenge from my control

But when at last she, acquiescent, lay
  In the sweet-scented shadow of the firs,
Lovely and broken, granting—asking—all,
  It was *his* eyes I met: not hers—not hers!

\* \* \*

Three months I waited: all the village talked,
  And ever anxiously she urged our flight.
Yet still I lingered, till her beauty paled,
  And wearily she came to me at night.

Then, seeing Love, subservient to Revenge,
  Had well achieved his own creative end,
And in his work must soon be manifest,
  Compassing thus my duty to my friend,

One tranquil, sultry night I rode away
    Till far behind the purple hills were dim,
Exulting in my spirit, "Thus I leave
    Her to her fate, and my revenge to him!"

Swiftly he struck her, her lord; the body lay
    With hacked-off breasts, dishonoured, in the Pass.
Months later, riding lonely through the gorge,
    I saw it still, among the long-grown grass.

It was well done; my soul is satisfied.
    Friendship is sweet, and Love is sweeter still,
But Vengeance has a savour all its own—
    A strange delight—well known to those who kill.

Such was the story Afzul told to me,
    While wood-fires crackled in the evening breeze,
And blows on hammered tent-pegs stirred the air
    Sweet with the fragrance from the Sinjib trees.

Tent-like, above, up-held by jagged peaks,
    The heavy purple of the tranquil sky
Shed its oft-broken promises of peace,
    While twinkling stars bemocked the worn-out lie!

## Nay, Not To-night

NAY, not to-night;—the slow, sad rain is falling
   Sorrowful tears, beneath a grieving sky,
Far off a famished jackal, faintly calling,
   Renders the dusk more lonely with its cry.

The mighty river rushes, sobbing, seawards,
   The shadows shelter faint mysterious fears,
I turn mine eyes for consolation theewards,
   And find thy lashes tremulous with tears.

If some new soul, asearch for incarnation,
   Should, through our kisses, enter Life again,
It would inherit all our desolation,
   All the soft sorrow of the slanting rain.

When thou desirest Love's supreme surrender,
   Come while the morning revels in the light,
Bulbuls around us, passionately tender,
   Singing among the roses red and white.

Thus, if it be my sweet and sacred duty,
   Subservient to the Gods' divine decree,

To give the world again thy vivid beauty,
  I should transmit it with my joy in thee.

I could not if I would, Beloved, deceive thee.
  Wouldst thou not feel at once a feigned caress?
Yet, do not rise, I would not have thee leave me,
  My soul needs thine to share its loneliness.

Let the dim starlight, when the low clouds sunder,
  Silver the perfect outline of thy face.
Such faces had the saints; I only wonder
  That thine has sought my heart for resting-place

## The Dying Prince

THERE are no days for me any more, for the dawn is dark with tears,
There is no rest for me any more, for the night is thick with fears,
There are no flowers nor any fruit, for the sorrowful locusts came,
And the garden is but a memory, the vineyard only a name.

There is no light in the empty sky, no sail upon the sea,
Birds are yet on their nests perchance, but they sing no more to me.
Past—vanished—faded away—all the joys that were.
My youth died down in a swift decline when they married her to despair.

"My lord, the crowd in the Audience Hall; how long wilt thou have them wait?"
I have given my father's younger son the guidance of the State.
"The steeds are saddled, the Captains call for the orders of the day."
Tell them that I shall ride no more to the hunting or the fray.

"Sweet the scent of the Moghra flowers"; Brother, it may be so.
"The young, flushed spring is with us again." Is it? I did not know.
"The Zamorin's daughter draweth near, on slender golden feet";
Oh, a curse upon all sweet things say I, to whom they are no more sweet!

Dost think that a man as sick as I can compass a woman's ease?
That the sons of a man who is like to me could ever find rest or peace?
Tell them to marry them where they will, if their longing be so sore,
Such are the things that all men seek, but I shall seek no more.

All my muscles are fallen in, and the blood deserts my veins,
Every fibre and bone of me is waxen full of pains,
The iron feet of mine enemy's curse are heavy upon my head,
Look at me and judge for thyself, thou seest I am but dead.

"Then, who is it, Prince, who has done this thing, has sown such a bitter seed,
That we hale him forth to the Market-place, bind him and let him bleed,

That the flesh may shudder and wince and writhe, reddening 'neath the rod."
Love is the evil-doer, alas! and how shalt thou scourge a God?

## The Hut

Dear little Hut by the rice-fields circled
  That cocoa-nuts shade above.
I hear the voices of children singing,
  And that means love.

When shall the traveller's march be over,
  When shall his wandering cease?
This little homestead is bare and simple,
  And that means peace.

Nay! to the road I am not unfaithful;
  In tents let my dwelling be!
I am not longing for Peace or Passion
  From any one else but thee,
      My Krishna,
  Any one else but thee!

## My Paramour Was Loneliness

My paramour was loneliness
    And lying by the sea,
Soft songs of sorrow and distress
    He did beget in me.

Later another lover came
    More meet for my desire,
"Radiant Beauty" was his name;
    His sons had wings of fire!

*My Paramour Was Loneliness*

## The Rice Was Under Water

The Rice was under water, and the land was scourged with rain,
The nights were desolation, and the day was born in pain.
Ah, the famine and the fever and the cruel, swollen streams,
I had died, except for Krishna, who consoled me—in my dreams!

The Burning-Ghats were smoking, and the jewels melted down,
The Temples lay deserted, for the people left the town.
Yet I was more than happy, though passing strange it seems,
For I spent my nights with Krishna, who loved me—in my dreams!

## "Surface Rights"

Drifting, drifting down the River,
  Tawny current and foam-flecked tide,
Sorrowful songs of lonely boatmen,
  Mournful forests on either side.

Thine are the outcrops' glittering blocks,
  The quartz where the rich pyrites gleam,
The golden treasure of unhewn rocks
  And the loose gold in the stream.

But,—the dim vast forests along the shore,
  That whisper wonderful things o' nights
These are things that I value more,
  My beautiful "surface rights."

Drifting, drifting down the River,—
  Stars a-tremble about the sky—
Ah, my lover, my heart is breaking,
  Breaking, breaking, I know not why.

Why is Love such a sorrowful thing?
  This I never could understand;

Pain and passion are linked together,
  Ever I find them hand in hand.

Loose thy hair in its soft profusion,
  Let thy lashes caress thy cheek,—
These are the things that express thy spirit,
  What is the need to explain or speak?

Drifting, drifting along the River,
  Under the light of a wan low moon,
Steady, the paddles; Boatmen, steady,—
  Why should we reach the sea so soon?

See where the low spit cuts the water,
  What is that misty wavering light?
Only the pale datura flowers
  Blossoming through the silent night.

What is the fragrance in thy tresses?
  'T is the scent of the champa's breath;
The meaning of champa bloom is passion—
  And of datura—death!

Sweet are thy ways and thy strange caresses
  That sear as flame, and exult as wine.
But I care only for that wild moment
  When my soul arises and reaches thine.

Wistful voices of wild birds calling—
  Far, faint lightning towards the West,—

Twinkling lights of a Tyah homestead,—
  Ruddy glow on a girl's bare breast—

Drifting boats on a mournful River,
  Shifting thoughts in a dreaming mind,—
We two, seeking the Sea, together,—
  When we reach it,—what shall we find?

# *Shivratri (the Night of Shiva)*
(While the procession passed at Ramesram)

    Nearer and nearer cometh the car
      Where the Golden Goddess towers,
    Sweeter and sweeter grows the air
      From a thousand trampled flowers.
    We two rest in the Temple shade
      Safe from the pilgrim flood,
    This path of the Gods in olden days
      Ran royally red with blood.

    Louder and louder and louder yet
      Throbs the sorrowful drum—
    That is the tortured world's despair,
      Never a moment dumb.
    Shriller and shriller shriek the flutes,
      Nature's passionate need—
    Paler and paler grow my lips,
      And still thou bid'st them bleed.

    Deeper and deeper and deeper still,
      Never a pause for pain—

Darker and darker falls the night
    That golden torches stain.
Closer, ah! closer, and still more close
    Till thy soul reach my soul—
Further, further, out on the tide
    From the shores of self-control.

Glowing, glowing, to whitest heat,
    Thy feverish passions burn,
Fiercer and fiercer, cruelly fierce,
    To thee my senses yearn.
Fainter and fainter runs my blood
    With desperate fight for breath—
This, my Beloved, thou sayest is Love,
    Or I should have deemed it Death!

## The First Wife

Ah, my lord, are the tidings true,
That thy mother's jewels are shapen anew?

I hear that a bride has chosen been,
The stars consulted, the parents seen.

Had I been childless, had never there smiled
The brilliant eyes from the face of a child,

Then at least I had understood
This thing they tell me thou findest good.

But I have been down to the River of Death,
With painful footsteps and shuddering breath

Seven times; thou hast daughters three,
And four young sons who are fair as thee.

I am not unlovely, over my head
Not twenty summers as yet have sped.

'T is eleven years since my opening life
Was given to thee by my father's wife.

Ah, those days—they were lovely to me,
When little and shy I waited for thee.

Till I locked my arms round my lover above,
A child in form but a woman in love.

And I bore thy sons, as a woman should,
Year by year, as is meet and good.

Thy mother was ever content with me—
And oh, Beloved, I worshipped thee!

And now it's over; alas, my lord,
Better I felt thy sharpest sword.

I hear she is youthful and fair as I
When I came to thee in the days gone by.

Her breasts are firmer; this bosom slips
Somewhat, weighted by children's lips.

But they were thy children. Oh, lord my king
Ah, why hast thy heart devised this thing?

I am not as the women of this thy land,
Meek and timid, broken to hand.

From the distant North I was given to thee,
Whose daughters are passionate, fierce and free.

I could not dwell by a rival's side,
I seek a bridegroom, as thou a bride.

The night she yieldeth her youth to thee
Death shall take his pleasure in me.

## I Arise and Go Down to the River

I ARISE and go down to the River, and currents that come
                                                    from the sea,
Still fresh with the salt of the ocean, are lovely and precious
                                                           to me,
The waters are silver and silent, except where the kingfisher
                                                           dips,
Or the ripples wash off from my shoulder the reddening stain
                                                    of thy lips.

Two things make my joy at this moment: thy gold-coloured
                                                beauty by night,
And the delicate charm of the River, all pale in the day-
                                                breaking light,
So cool are the waters' caresses. Ah, which is the lovelier,—
                                                           this?
Or the fire that it kindles at midnight, beneath the soft glow
                                                    of thy kiss?

Ah, Love has a mighty dominion, he forges with passionate
                                                         breath
The links which stretch out to the Future, with forces of life
                                                  and of death,

*I Arise and Go Down to the River*

But great is the charm of the River, so soft is the sigh of the reeds,
They give me, long sleepless from passion, the peace that my weariness needs.
I float on the breast of my River, and startle the birds on the edge,
To land on a newly found island, a boat that is caught in the sedge,
The rays of the sun are still level, not yet has the heat of the day
Deflowered the mists of the morning, that linger in delicate grey.

What land was his dwelling whose fancy first gave unto Paradise birth?
He never had swum in my River, or else he had fixed it on earth!
Oh, grace of the palm-tree reflections, oh, sense of the wind from the sea!
Oh, divine and serene exultation of one who is lonely and free!

Ah, delicate breezes of daybreak, so scentless, refreshing and free!
And yet—had my midnight been lonely you had been less lovely to me.
This coolness comes laden with solace, because I am hot from the fire,
As often devotion to virtue arises from sated desire.

*Gautama came forth from his Palace; he felt the night wind on his face,*
*He loathed, as he left, the embraces, the softness and scent of the place,*
*But, ah, if his night had been loveless, with no one to solace his need,*
*He never had written that sermon which men so devotedly read.*

Ah, River, thy gentle persuasion; I doubt if I seek any more
The beauty that hurts me and holds me beneath the low roof on the shore.
I loved thee, ay, loved—for a season, but thou, was it love or desire,
The glow of the Sun in his glory, or only the heat of a fire?

I think not that thou wilt regret me, for thou art too joyous and fair,
So many are keen to caress thee, thy passionate midnights to share.
Thou wilt not have time to remember, before a new love-knot is tied,
The stranger who loved thee and left thee, who drifted away on the tide.

Two things I have found that are lovely, though most things are sullen and grey;
One: Peace—but what mortal has found him; and Passion—but when would he stay?

So I shall return to my River, and floating at ease on its
 breast,
Shall find, what Love never has given—a sense of most in-
 finite rest.

When the years have gone by and departed, what thought
 shall I keep of this land?
A curl of thy waist-reaching tresses? a flower received from
 thy hand?
Nay, if I can fathom the future, I fancy my relic will be
Some shell, my beloved one, the River has stol'n from the
 store of the sea.

## Listen, Beloved

Listen, Beloved, the Casurinas quiver,
    Each tassel prays the wind to set it free,
Hark to the frantic sobbing of the river,
    Wild to attain extinction in the sea.
All Nature blindly struggles to dissolve
In other forms and forces, thus to solve
The painful riddle of identity.
Ah, that my soul might lose itself in thee!

Yet, my Beloved One, wherefore seek I union,
    Since there is no such thing in all the world,—
Are not our spirits linked in close communion,—
    And on my lips thy clinging lips are curled?
Thy tender arms are round my shoulders thrown,
I hear thy heart more loudly than my own,
And yet, to my despair, I know thee far,
As in the stellar darkness, star from star.

Even in times when love with bounteous measure
    A simultaneous joy on us has shed,
In the last moment of delirious pleasure,
    Ere the sense fail, or any force be fled,

My rapture has been even as a wall,
Shutting out any thought of thee at all!
My being, by its own delight possessed,
Forgot that it was sleeping on thy breast.

Ay, from his birth each man is vowed and given
    To a vast loneliness, ungauged, unspanned,
Whether by pain and woe his soul be riven,
    Or all fair pleasures clustered 'neath his hand.
His gain by day, his ecstasy by night,—
His force, his folly, fierce or faint delight,—
Suffering or sorrow, fortune, feud, or care,—
Whate'er he find or feel,—he may not share.

Lonely we join the world, and we depart
    Even as lonely, having lived alone,
The breast that feeds us, the beloved one's heart
    The lips we kiss,—or curse—alike unknown.
Ay, even these lips of thine, so often kissed,
What certitude have I that they exist?
Alas, it is the truth, though harsh it seems,
I have been loved as sweetly in my dreams.

Therefore if I should seem too fiercely fond,
    Too swift to love, too eager to attain,
Forgive the fervour that would forage beyond
    The limits set to mortal joy and pain.
Knowing the soul's unmeasured loneliness,

My passion must be mingled with distress,
As I, despairing, struggle to draw near
What is as unattainable as dear.

Thirst may be quenched at any kindly river,
    Rest may be found 'neath any arching tree.
No sleep allures, no draughts of love deliver
    My spirit from its aching need of thee.
Thy sweet assentiveness to my demands,
All the caressive touches of thy hands,—
These soft cool hands, with fingers tipped with fire,—
They can do nothing to assuage desire.

Sometimes I think my longing soul remembers
    A previous love to which it aims and strives,
As if this fire of ours were but the embers
    Of some wild flame burnt out in former lives.
Perchance in earlier days I *did* attain
That which I seek for now so all in vain,
Maybe my soul with thine *was* fused and wed
In some great night, long since dissolved and dead.

We may progress; but who shall answer clearly
    The riddle of the endless change of things.
Perchance in other days men loved more dearly,
    Or Love himself had wider ways and wings,
Maybe we gave ourselves with less control,
Or simpler living left more free the soul,

So that with ease the flesh aside was flung,—
Or was it merely that *Mankind was young?*

Or has my spirit a divine prevision
    Of vast vague passions stored in days to be,
When some strong souls shall conquer their division
    And two shall be as one, eternally?
Finding at last upon each other's breast,
Unutterable calm and infinite rest,
While love shall burn with so intense a glow
That both shall die, and neither heed or know.

Why do I question thus, and wake confusion
    In the soft thought that lights thy perfect face,
Ah, shed once more thy perfumed hair's profusion,
    Open thine arms and make my resting place.
Lay thy red lips on mine as heretofore,
Grant me the treasure of thy beauty's store,
Stifle all thought in one imperious kiss,—
What shall I ask for more than this,— and this?

## Oh, Unforgotten and Only Lover

Oh, unforgotten and only lover,
    Many years have swept us apart,
But none of the long dividing seasons
    Slay your memory in my heart.
In the clash and clamour of things unlovely
    My thoughts drift back to the times that were
When I, possessing thy pale perfection,
    Kissed the eyes and caressed the hair.

Other passions and loves have drifted
    Over this wandering, restless soul,
Rudderless, chartless, floating always
    With some new current of chance control.
But thine image is clear in the whirling waters—
    Ah, forgive—that I drag it there,
For it is so part of my very being
    That where I wander it too must fare.

Ah, I have given thee strange companions,
    To thee—so slender and chaste and cool—
But a white star loses no glimmer of beauty
    In all the mud of a miry pool

That holds the grace of its white reflection;
    Nothing could fleck thee, nothing could stain,
Thou hast made a home for thy delicate beauty
    Where all things peaceful and lovely reign.

Doubtless the night that my soul remembers
    Was a sin to thee, and thine only one.
Thou thinkest of it, if thou thinkest ever,
    As a crime committed, a deed ill done.
But for me, the broken, the desert-dweller,
    Following Life through its underways,—
I know if those midnights thou hadst not granted
    I had not lived through these after days.

And that had been well for me; all would say so,
    What have I done since I parted from thee?
But things that are wasted, and full of ruin,
    All unworthy, even of me.
Yet, it was to me that the gift was given,
    No greater joy have the Gods above,—
That night of nights when my only lover,
    Though all reluctant, granted me love.

For thy beauty was mine, and my spirit knows it,
    Never, ah, never my heart forgets,
One thing fixed, in the torrent of changing,
    Faults and follies and fierce regrets.
Thine eyes and thy hair, that were lovely symbols
    Of that white soul that their grace enshrined,

They are part of me and my life for ever,
    In every fibre and cell entwined.

Men might argue that having known thee
    I had grown faithful and pure as thee,
Had turned at the touch of thy grace and glory
    From the average pathways trodden by me.
Hadst thou been kinder or I been stronger
    It may be even these things had been—
But one thing is clear to my soul for ever,
    I owe my owning of thee to sin.

Had I been colder I had not reached thee,
    Besmirched the ermine, beflecked the snow—
It was only sheer and desperate passion
    That won thy beauty in years ago.
And not for the highest virtues in Heaven,
    The utmost grace that the soul can name,
Would I resign what the sin has brought me,
    Which I hold glory, and thou—thy shame.

I talk of sin in the usual fashion,
    But God knows what is a sin to me—
We love more fiercely or love more faintly—
    But I doubt if it matters how these things be.
The best and the worst of us all sink under—
    What I held passion and thou held'st lust—
What name will it find in a few more seasons,
    When we both dissolve in an equal dust?

If a God there be, and a God seems needed
   To make the beauty of things like thee,
He doubtless also, some careless moment,
   Mixed the forces that fashioned me.
Also He, for His own good reason—
   Though I care little how these things are—
Gave me thee, in those few brief midnights,
   And that one solace He never can mar.

Ah me, the stars of such varying heavens
   Have watched me, under such alien skies,
Lay thy beauty naked before me
   To soothe and solace my world-worn eyes.
For one good gift to me has been given—
   A memory accurate, clear and keen,
That holds the vision, perfect for ever
   In charm and glory, of things once seen.

So I hold thee there, and my fancy wanders
   To each known beauty and blue-veined place,
I know how each separate eyelash trembles,
   And every shadow that sweeps thy face.
And this is a joy of which none can rob me,
   This is a pleasure that none can mar—
As sweet as thou wert, in that long past midnight
   Even as lovely my memories are.

Ah, unforgotten and only lover,
   If ever I drift across thy thought,

As even a vision unloved, unlovely,
    May cross the fancy, uncalled, unsought,
When the years that pass thee have shown, in passing
    That my love, *in its strength at least,* was rare—
Wilt thou not think—ah, hope of the hopeless—
    E'en as thou wouldst not, thou wilt not—care!

## Early Love

Who says I wrong thee, my half-opened rose?
Little he knows of thee or me, or love.—
I am so tender of thy fragile youth,
Yea, in my hours of wildest ecstasy,
Keeping close-bitted each careering sense.
Only I give mine eyes unmeasured law
To feed them where they will, and *their* delight
Was curbed at first, until thy tender shame
Died in the bearing of thy first born joy.

I am not cruel, my half-opened rose,
Though in the sunshine of my own desire
I have uncurled thy petals to the light
And fed the tendrils of thy dawning sense
With delicate caresses, till they leave
Thee tremulous with the newness of thy joy,
Sharing thy lover's fire with innocent flame.

Others will wrong thee, that I well foresee,
Being a man, knowing my fellow men,
And they who, knowing, would blame my love of thee
Contentedly will see thy beauty given,

When the world judges thou art ripe to wed,—
To the rough rites of marriage, to the pain
And grievous weariness of child-getting.—
This shall be right and licit in their eyes—
But it would break my heart, were I alive.

Yea, this will be; many will doubtless share
The rose whose bud has been my one delight,
And I shall not be there to shield my flower.
Yet, I have taught thee of the ways of men,
Much I have learnt in cities and in courts,
Winnowed to suit thy tender brain,—is thine,
Thus Life shall find thee, not all unprepared
To face its callous, subtle cruelties.

Still,—it will profit little; I discern
Thou art of those whose love will prove their curse
—Thou sayest thou lovest me, to thy delight?
Nay, little one, it is not love as yet.
Dear as thou art, and lovely, thou canst not love,
Thy later loves shall show the truth of this.

Ay, by some subtle signs I know full well
That thou art capable of that great love
Whose glory has the light of unknown heavens,
And makes hot Hell for those who harbour it.

Naught I can say could save thee from thyself,
Ah, were I half my age! Yet even that,

Had been too old for thy sweet thirteenth year.
Still, thou art happy now, and glad thine eyes,
When, as the lilac evening gains the sky,
I lay thee, 'twixt thine own soft hair and me,
Kissing thy senses into soft delight.
Ruffling the petals of my half-closed rose
With tender touches, and perpetual care
That no wild moment of mine own delight
Deep in the flower's heart,—should set the fruit.

Ah, in the days to come, it well may be,
When thou shalt see thy beauty stained and torn
By the harsh sequel of some future love,
Thy thoughts shall stray to thy first lover's grave,
And thou shalt murmur, "Ay, but that was love.
They were most wrong who said he did me wrong
Only I was too young to understand."

# Vayu the Wind

Ah, Wind, I have always loved thee
    Since those far off nights
When I lay beneath the vines
    A prey to strange delights,
For among my tresses
Thy soft caresses
    Were sweet as a lover's to me.

Later thou grewest more wanton, or I more shy,
And after the bath I drew my garments close,
Fearing thy soft persuasion amongst my hair,
When thou camest fresh with the scent of some ruffled rose

Ah, Wind, thou hast lain with the Desert,
    I know her savour well,
  And the spices wherewith she scents her breasts—
She who has known such countless lovers
Yet rarely borne a city among her sands—
    Thou comest as one from a night of love,
        Thy breath is broken and hard,—
    Bringing echoes of lonely things,
        Vast and cruel, that the soft and golden sands
        Buried beneath thin ripples so long ago.

Ah, Wind, thou hast given me lovely things,
    The scent of a thousand flowers,
And the heavy perfume of pollen-laden fields,
Strange snatches of wild song from the heart of the dark
                                   Bazaar
    That thrilled to my very core,
Till I threw the sheet aside and rose to follow,—
    But whither, or what?

Also, Wind, thou broughtest the breath of the sea,
    The sound of its myriad waves.
And in nights when I lay on the lonely sands
Stretching mine arms to thee,
    Thou gavest me something—faint and vast and sweet,
Something ineffable, wistful, from far away,
      Elsewhere—Beyond—

And thou wast kind to me in my times of love,
    Cooling my lips
    That my lover wore away,
While, wafting the scent from his divided hair,
    Thou show'dst the stars between
Far away, and eclipsed by his burning eyes
      Even the stars.

And now I almost foresee the place and the hour
    When I shall open my dying lips to thee
      And receive a last cool kiss.

Afterwards, Wind, since I have always loved thee,—
    Whirl my dust to the scented heart of a moghra flower
      *His* flower, but, ah, thou knowest,—
    So often thy kisses have mingled with his and mine

Printed in the United Kingdom
by Lightning Source UK Ltd.
9548900001B